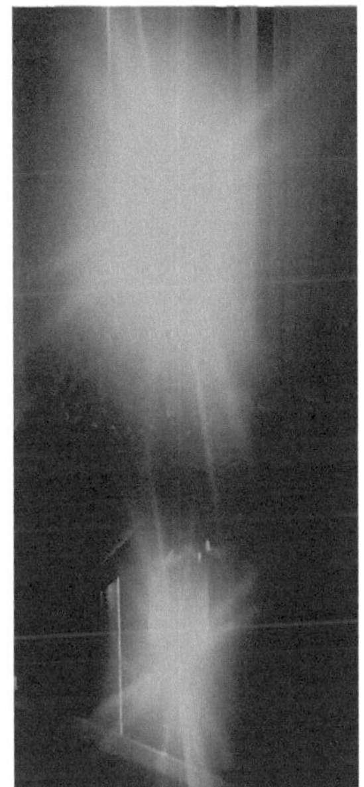

Love First

Scribed by

Tym Dee

Published by New Generation Publishing in 2020

First Edition

Paperback ISBN: 978-1-80031-661-4
Ebook ISBN: 978-1-80031-660-7

www.newgeneration-publishing.com

New Generation Publishing

Introduction

While reflecting upon his life one day with its varied scenarios and regrets, the scribe for this book became aware in a single moment of a simple realisation, of a connecting common theme within disappointments and failures. That Love had always been absent particularly when reviewing those scenes relating to relationships, life dreams and projects. In the next moment, arrived the thought, what if Love had been placed back then, as the First intention and goal in each scenario? Yes, it was thought, the scene would have been a lot happier. Certainly more success. The world itself was then considered along with its wars and orphans, political conflicts, greed and shortages, discord and lies. What is Love had been placed first and maintained first. Not kept absent. The vision came again of there being more successes, peace, less death and tears. More 'win-win' for all involved, more permanently too. Right now, what if nations and their leaders would also put Love forward as their first intent in any dealing? Imagine . . .

This scribe, reviewing his own life again with all its wrong decisions and implications that had lasted on further for decades often, paths taken with such effort and expense that so often led nowhere, or to another path that was again absent of Love and common success. The river of thought progressed, recalling times when, with all options tried and hope gone. In final desperation, the Creator had to be finally acknowledged, prayed to, Asked out loud even, for solutions and resolutions to appear. Again, what if the Creator had been Asked of First when faced with a decision, a new venture, relationship and pathway in Life?

Tired of the misery caused to everyone including his self and - in trepidation of causing more, a decision was inspired and made. To do the opposite of what had been done before – to live life putting Love First in intent, thoughts, action and with any type of decision expended. From moving countries to driving a car, certainly daily work and family. Vowing regardless of how good schemes looked at the start, to Ask of the Creator, first. First, before taking any first steps when starting out on any venture or taking a decision that would affect anybody else around or living thing. It became clear now, In retrospect, that every decision, choice, emotional state, word even thought – always, but always affected everybody. Over time it seemed, everything in the immediate world, at least.

It was considered initially to an extent, an experiment. That by engineering Love as a First consideration and motive, thinking the very best not for 'Me' ,but ' We', would perhaps give more positivity to our life's ventures and daily interactions.

Then, a moment of realisation, a sense of imprinted knowing appeared and now stayed. In minutes and subsequent months, more 'understandings' appeared. Often daily. Inspirations regarding universal Love, Love viewed as an energy owned by everyone and its origins with the Creator, appeared and stayed. These understandings and wisdoms became imbued into the mind, as if they had always been there.

These deemed 'wisdoms' gently, yet unrelentingly demanded to be written and shared. They are now duly here in this book written as a discourse as inferred and received for You to also consider and gain benefit.

This book was written as carefully as possible to ensure that the information passed through the scribe was not from any conjuring within the mind. It was insisted upon that the peculiar seemingly improper use of capital letters and punctuations be maintained. They carried importance to inferred meanings. When the realisations appeared, they accompanied a signature rush of Love, a profound peace and a power that melted his core. It caused tears of joy to flow quite often.

The messages were alive. They linked constantly to themes of being conscious of unconditional Love (not that often associated with sentimentality, emotionalism or lust). They required not to remain a feeling, but to be considered an energy applicable to daily life. It's noticeable practical application very evident if applied First and daily as a prerequisite to a decision, meeting or action.

A further theme and undercurrent related through was that of the earth to be considered a school and theatrical stage. A stage for learning about Love and for all to reflect that all life could be considered drama, set up to create learning and mastery of the Great Lesson of Love and their own rediscovery of its Source.

The inspirations received came with one insistence, that now in this epoch; the Creator be acknowledged. Acknowledged as the sustainer of life in our every moment and with All, simultaneousely. That the reader takes up the challenge. To interact with that energy from which born out of. The challenge, the dare to use Love First in each day.

Here verbal words fail, but may this book speak to you too. May the reader experience this Love along the path of discovering your own uniqueness and use of the energy of Love as always, First.

Preface

Why produce a book about Love, yet another one? Earth based emotionality, distinct from the Love emanating into and from a Soul, is inferred throughout this book. Love, transcending the physical, is still being sung about, lamented of and acted upon stages and film sets in all manner of scenarios - now and from ancient times, albeit more often in a romantic context. Love referred to in a spiritual and religious context, certainly for the last 2,000 years where it is considered a pinnacle of human experience and interaction with The Creator and fellow souls.

In the present era, deemed channelled and received wisdoms from entities, the Creator, Angels and aliens etc., appear prolific. The scribe of **this** book (not the considered Author) offers . . . yet another one for You.

This book adheres to no particular religion, though the truths offered within, may be noticed to reassuringly 'dovetail' with much already written around spiritual love. Truth to be Truth, has to naturally 'dovetail' (using carpentry terminology), the endorsement of any deemed universal Truth, though with the explicating interpretations varying, perhaps only for You, perhaps for others that are now with You as well. For those adhering to a chosen religion, it is hoped that this book of inspirations will always help enhance and exalt Your own faith.

This book regarding Love carried during its compilation a feeling of urgency, a true need to bring it into lives and the world, perhaps in order to assist now we may survive here. In the reading of this book, it may help to see and feel oneself as a member of All Creation, in All Ways, Always.

This book is written to be dipped into, even upon impetus, in preference to reading from cover to cover. Dipped into whenever inspired, or when carried on a journey or commute. Perhaps, hidden within a glove compartment or bedside drawer. It may be offered to the person opposite, if felt that an inspiration right for that moment, waits.

In part, a manual. Its observations and deemed truths referred to daily. Within this book, Love and The Creator are deemed to be one and the same, however perceived.

It is hoped that when dipping into the book, the inspirations read read, may be just right for You at that particular time in Your life, in whatever scenario You may be currently in and evolving out from.

This book has been considered to be alive and may indeed speak to you through the pages when with sincerity, you Ask of it.

The grammar with its seemingly unorthodox capital letters and combined words have been purposely requested to be retained as they are, for it is deemed they add meaning, power and poignancy to these inspired statements, from wherever in Creation they may have originated.

This book is offered to You, for inspiration and possible seeds for new understandings and possibilities. With this book You may read it, shelve it, pass it on or discard. Over to You. The scribe humbly asks only one thing of You; that perhaps You may acknowledge even for a few seconds the Source of All that made possible the scribe, the paper for the book, Your eyes, breathe and heartbeat to create You and sustain You here on this planet, in order to read it and further provide energy to put this book later - into Your bag . . . or a bin.

Perhaps the reader may like to ponder their own use of Love (not lust) energy –noting scientifically its effect, immediately and also over time. It asks the reader, to note results in their lives from their new intent to project Love, First.

It is felt strongly now that our earth home is very necessarily now becoming a totally 'Creator friendly, Creator aware' planet. Why It is often considered, should The Creator continue to tolerate and accommodate those that clearly have awareness of their Creator, yet choose to ignore the Creator, refuse to Love, plunder the planet's gifts and fruits and offer back little more than pollution and ill will. Within times now coming, that question may be answered.

Received Inspirations and Discourses on Love

Everything and everyone in the Universe, responds to Love.

ঞ

If Love is put 2nd, suffering comes in 1st.

ঞ

Love is given and received exactly the same. Whether having a physical body to experience the world and move around in – or not. Love is constant, beyond matter.

ঞ

Your world, indeed Your Universe, may transform to a playground in place of a penitentiary, with moments of daily Love and gratitude to Your Source.

ঞ

Your total permanent happiness, wholeness and completeness are inevitable. With Love. . . it will be faster.

ঞ

Love First - All . . . less You Fall.

ঞ

Love is the grand investment expressed in the moment of Now, yet importantly and most certainly - within Your Forever.

ঞ

In deciding to live Your life, maybe Your Forever by putting Love First, Your intent , Your decision alone is enough to create instant change You may now notice already. . . . . .

Forgiving All, with Love for All – health and vitality flourishes.

You are the same now – as when You are (by current belief) – 'dead' An extension of Source as before birth and Now. Living within Your Forever. Physical costumes and their accompanying personas, by necessity change to benefit Your learning and growth upon the earth school stage; but never You.

Love is within this book and an experience of The Source - Your Source of Life, which formed You , sustains You here – in every moment of Now.

We not Me . . . carries inherently within that phrase, as performed with sincere intent, that Love is given First place.

The Creator, from observation, appears to think in the context of WE, not ME. For that alone, all may be grateful. May You adopt that way of being too.

Within the experience perceived as Love is the experience of the Creator so very close and within, always there.

A Divine Soul, You cannot but help radiate Life energy, Love energy. Transmit Your Love to just one person, yet others may feel it too. What You send is Universal. Is instant.

Love will by its inherent nature forgives in the end when the lesson is learnt and another step achieved upon Your unique pathway within Your Forever.

In acknowledgement of the Source daily, You cease being the slave of the physical finite body and earth bound sensations; opening to a greater realm of sensations, experiences and possibilities that the real You always sought.

To Love First is a decision made by Your whole being – whether for 0.100 of a second or less, or 3 hours or more; it matters not. Sincere intention is only asked. Prophet or servant, it matters not, All are of the One Life Force and Source whose Love You share when You Love.

As a finger nail paring is to the remainder of Your body, so earthly bodies are to a greater self. Bodies facilitate experience upon the earth school. Most will miss their bodies the second after death as much as missing a finger nail paring after a manicure. The body - a small extension of Your soul as a finger nail is to the body.

Something not working, send Love to it. Yet still it does not work . . . . send more Love. Everything in Creation, responds to Love, Everything, everyone responds.

Human sourced Love, once free of the infatuation stage, lust exhausted, then may leave Love retained, or else the relationship may not continue alone. Do not the relationships romantic, business or those based upon a common interest seem to last with stability and evolution?

Not hold back Your Love within, while You wait for that person, that day, when they may possibly, sometime - arrive. Just now, right now - pour out Your Love, but not as an act of bartering for Your dream. Pour it out asking nothing in return, just like the very nature of Love itself. Your dream, that person, that thing, that scenario may find You quicker! Pour forth Love, yet not emotion, not passion, not sensuality, joint influencing powers, just pure Love. Pure Love recognises itself.

Love seeds joy.

With Love, from its infinite unlimited Source, does it travel, with Infinite Intelligence, releasing the perfect solution ensuring progress to the next step and unfurling of Your next petal.

Dear soul, may You appreciate and give thanks to Your Source, this benevolent single supreme energy that powers all Creation with supreme Love. It is an energy understood and responded to by all life , by all matter, by all other off energy derived from off of the One.

With Love from its infinite unlimited Source travelling with infinite unlimited intelligence, it may be observed on occasions, results can be immediate.

In the absence of Love, learning and experience continue. In the absence of Love, the learning continues to reinforce and confirm . . . Love is Life, Love is All.

Love in its essence carries gratitude and appreciation, for within its rays we perhaps feel and remember our original heritage that incorporates the idea of perfect wholeness and harmony.

A prescribed application of Love, may negate pain now.

Everything emanating from within the light of Your Source – is perceived to constantly seeking repair to wholeness and balance. The soul seeks it, the body seeks it in a small way or by complete renewal. All are of Spirit. Some encapsulated, interacting through physical form. Developing wisdom, strengths, discovering new joys. Whether in or out of a body, it matters not to the Creator. You are constantly loved throughout Forever. The death of the physical costume, may be considered an improvement, a restoration, and repair back to wholeness. The Source wants your happy wholeness.

Bringing in Love through Your Self endorses and instigates a process of restoration to your living wholeness as permanently perceived by the Creator.

The key indication of Love, the 'acid test' - is for the total absence of need for anything in return. Love carries sufficient payment inherently within itself.

Emitting Love to one; yet all Life feels Your emanation too.

When linked with Source in trust and communication, a migration begins away from earth victim and towards reclaiming Your power, in turn becoming also a transformer.

Dramas lived without putting Love First, without acknowledgement of the Creator, may bring loneliness. In that space and time, it may be naturally pondered; how perhaps by placing Love First, it would not ever occur. With Love First in Your life, You stay away from that condition, Forever .

With Love, All grows and purifies. Without Love, dissolution until Love finds it again.

Life Dramas = Life Lessons About Love. Lessons about when Love is not First and the Source remembered. Violence dramas offer a vehement example. The understanding of Love First if not grasped, increases the intensity of further dramas here at earth school until the Great Lesson of Love is learnt.

Without Love present in any relationship or venture, dissolution and dismay follow. This remains until Love is allowed to be made present and placed First.

You have Love in You, now. Some reason that without Love from the Creator of All, nothing could exist. To exist, there is Love in some form. Love a Divine Spark and the Spark of Life.

When You put Love First, faith is automatic.

If Love brings the fruit of Joy, so MinusLove brings the fruit of Learning.

Remember, You have chosen to be at this gymnasium, the exercises to master, together with Your instructor, before entering. Nothing to be gained if always easy. As agreed for The Good of All and progression, back in the reception area, located just outside, slightly to the side of the workout area. You chose this, before changing into costume. There is a viewing gallery to go to, when Your session is complete.

You walk to places and people where is the most Love. You run from places and people with MinusLove.

No mask or façade that purports to be of Love, is ever convincing. Love is real or not all.

Who, or what You do not Love, within time turns into hell - to remind - to use Love always.

Love opens doors. Send Love First to Your destination, Your meeting, before arrival. . . . then arrive.

One time, even now, You thought weakness, felt weak and insignificant? With a Love, that insists upon no payment, You are a proven power within Creation.

Live with Love as Your prime currency and means of exchange. It is the best investment and passport when travelling through Your magnificent Forever.

Send Love First, to Your cup . . . whatever You may fill it with.

Those that say while seeing a Loved one fade, daily and within hours, how can a loving Creator allow this? There is prayer, yet they suffer and fade. *The Creator, does not care* . . . is often thought. Perhaps, a new beautiful strong body awaits, close by, out of sight. Holding on, clinging in pain to the body as if an old coat, too worn to wear. Who is it now that does not care? The Source, sees only Your Forever as perfect, beyond the changing of earth suits.

To endorse a wonderful Forever of which is dreamt, may Love always right now be put First. May the best and first thing to Love First, be The Creator.

To restore, to forgive, is to allow others and things, to facilitate making a perfect accord with the original Divine idea.

Love behoves Love.

No years of celibacy, abstinence from provided earthly and bodily pleasures, mental exercises and devotional prayers while hidden from the world . . . are necessary. Just perhaps pure seconds of Your time, to sincerely acknowledge The Creator with Love, with reverence. Those that sincerely choose not to, may now in this epoch, face a future elsewhere.

Love is expressed and made visible by actions, never words or, smiling masks and gifts with no feeling. Never.

Recognise the people with MinusLove, for those who wear the mask of purported Love – by their eyes, touch and actions. Love, true Love, cannot be acted.

In Life, in Existence; All either move towards Love . . . or towards MinusLove.

Love guides a perfect journey.

With Love not First, greed by the few may appear seemingly in proportion to the lack experienced by many.

Love . . . .programmable? Only when using pure Love energy and intent.

Through putting Love First, before anything, anyone, even Yourself ; that the process of coming into awareness of Your Source, automatically begins.

Love will always win.

The Love 'feeling' is regarded by many to be a living experience of The Creator in the eternity called Now.

Interfering by thought, word or action with free will is a 'No-No' in the eyes of The Creator; when Love is applied First and always - it is perhaps always a safe 'Yes-Yes'.

Gratitude; performs the rounding of the circle, the completion of the square of life. Gratitude has Love inherent and demands expression. Gratitude is homage to the Giver behind all that is given. Gratitude with giving hands completes the act of delivering, by giving. The energy within giving radiating into infinity, links to itself, creating more, for the giver and receiver. The energy contained within an act of gratitude is of the Divine.

Keeping loving ' it ' or 'them '. Inevitably, It or Them . . . will start to glow with joy!

With putting Love First, the Creator is mimicked. Alignment occurs with the will of the Source of Life with its unlimited unfolding ongoing everywhere now.

Longer 'time' is spent in Forever than on the earth within the biological earth vehicles. The truly realistic worthwhile investments are for those ones that invest Love energy for a profitable return, within the Forever life.

Lack of health, money, respect, food, hope, water, mobility – can be traced back to the absence of Love. Love reinstated as First priority, transmutes lack back on to the road to Plenty.

With Love pure and untainted, there is no room for fear. All Love, the presence of The Creator, in action.

Ignorance harbours the most evil. Love lets You now sail free.

Part of Creation, You also are expanding and evolving; the time appears it seems, for All on earth for expanding thought frameworks, visioning not only being a member of a locality, country, planet or even galaxy - but a Universe,

Giving out with Love First, You also receive Love, knowingly or unknowingly the Source of Love and of Life within Your heart.

As actors and actresses here on earth, final scenes may conclude with Love sweeping in from the wings. Love, so often scripted to be held back, allows learning from having Love absent from the scenes of Your life, with the contrast of having it present.

As in life, absence of Love within a drama can leave disappointment, destruction, dismay. With Love arriving to the life stage; completion, happiness, solutions and resolutions follow to the final curtain, with great applause . . . and drying of tears.

Love is Your Source. You feel it, image it in Your heart area and beyond. It radiates and does not stop, ever. It never stops for all Forever. The stuff of the Universe. From Love, everything lasting was borne.

Radiating Love, by default You are a centre for a fresh wave of Love energy, with the thoughts carried within its wake. Love never ceases streaming from Your Source. You can stop electrical, radio wave, ocean wave energy, but not Love energy. It remains somewhere even with the shadow of hate.

Love transmutes with its touch, all that is lesser than itself.

Loving the Source of Love, First – You may feel Love return. With that Love You may be anything.

Transmute fear energy with Love.

You may transform any adverse moment back in - and throughout Your Forever, just apply Love.

Love energy, projected Love energy, shared with the same energy of Life that has and continues to create All, sustain All. Inherently, restoration to the original Divine Design is inevitable, Regardless of whether it is in Your mind or heart - or not. Whether You believe or not, it matters not – Love makes perfect.

In putting Love First, who should perhaps come First for our Love ? Maybe, the actual Source of Love could be a good start?

Ask, who drives Your life today, the decisions in each moment and joys? The body or the Soul? With Love and its energy, Your Soul. Without Love, Your body that is not Forever, but Your Soul . . .

Where there is pure Love there is Plenty, but for use – always and onwards only, with Love.

From the considered eye of The Creator. Illness, has known to manifest to parts shown MinusLove.

Send out Love to the intended pathway, before it is walked. Send Love to the ones You intend to meet – before You meet. Send Your Love to Your transaction, before it is performed. Send Love to that which You intend to create and give, before You create and give. Through these ways All also benefit for All are part of the All whether they are visible or not.

Love knows no boundaries within that which it touches and imbues.

Not see Yourself always, as a young human with a prime body age and condition; be not forlorn when years have passed, or yearn for those years to arrive when but young. With Love as a constant; see Yourself for all life as vital and complete, forever fun, forever growing up, enjoying all the different physical forms.

Express Love and Gratitude to money everywhere thinking of the amazing lasting good it will do Now and for All with the printed paper and metal coins, on and on and on and beyond.

Love, long associated with being an ingredient of a recipe for plenty, health and happiness.

If You are fading in this world, be assured You are preparing to be born again and elsewhere.

The 2 second Love projection? 1 second of pure total Love to Your Source, then 1 second of pure total Love out to the person, living thing, situation, memory, emotion or object that seeks your help with a return to balanced wholeness.

If in connection with the Source, MinusLove scenarios may be sustained - if You so choose.

A woman, a man - linking energies, combining in the touch of one hand upon another, a glance, an exchange of Love's energy, bringing the Divine to where You are now. A moment beyond mortal words, for most. The experience but a second, timeless and never forgotten.

Love restores – everything . . . .

With Love, Life can be seen as a lesson of Love in preference to one of penance.

Mammals, plants, birds, reptiles, trees, fish benefit from Love.

Love may be the 'stuff' of the Universe. It is the experience of many that from Love, anything lasting and of merit, is born.

Energy within daily work; as with all energy, comes from the One Source. Your core essence providing Life, movement and consciousness, continues into actions, whether You are paid or not paid. Energy radiated as a service becomes imbued and coloured with Love, with work transmuted to something Divine.

That which is not born of Love, is of Love and sustained by Love dissolves until it finds a form that allows it to become of Love; imbuing even more Love and Life.

With Love, connection and dialogue with the Source of Love and Life, could transform previous time spent in pain and punishment, now become time spent with joy and progress.

Love – the original and best 'Put Right' force.

Love highlights that being an atheist is possible for limited durations, within Your Forever.

Choosing to operate from the position of ME first; Loves in its essence comes 2nd or 3rd or never? Operating from WE first, Love, knowingly or unknowingly colours circumstances, aura and relationships and more. The first thing to evaporate may be loneliness.

When pure Love, Love without condition or any expectancy flows between two people, all things become added. Health, money, homes, friends, children, they flow when Love flows between two.

For Earth to become Heaven again as deemed originally; it is perhaps necessary only to Love as Your First intention, Your Source.

With Love, the world may become a playground, transmuting away from being a prison.

Heaven has no place for villains and liars, for those who refuse The Creator. The Source will not delete them, but move to what they have learned and earned in Love. They are still free to change, like You.

Love in pure form may be used to excess. Nothing else in the world can be engaged to excess that does not in the end, create harm . . . Just Love.

Human sourced Love, free of infatuation, lust exhausted, can leave Love retained, pure, or else not continue alone.

Whatever You Love - creates more of itself.

Heaven has no place for villains and liars, no place for those who refuse to acknowledge The Creator. The Source will not delete them, but only move to what they have learned and earned through Love. They have time to change. You have power to change now.

Love in pure form may be used to excess. Nothing else in the world can be engaged to excess that does not in the end, create harm. Just . . . Just Love.

Love is for All Forever. Never to stop, less everything not exist. Love demands to flow, to ebb and flow, be given and received, radiate as a sun, soaking Creation. It cannot be held back for long. Its appearance, the experience of it, is inevitable. Vital to the soul as a heartbeat to the physical body.

The common perception of the human being is of a physical body with consciousness attached. Perceptions may at times change to one of . . . pure consciousness with a physical body attached.

Love highlights that being an atheist is possible for limited durations, within Your Forever.

You are free to live with Love as Your prime currency even in the face of a wall of indifference and evil.

Love appears to exhibit a transforming power. Reflecting upon past experiences, has this not always been so?

Love pervades the Universe, everywhere, even within, around the darkest places and souls. Even dark places and souls cannot exist without some Love. Inherently creative, it knows only perfection.

With the conscious then automatic placing of Love as First, a decision to benefit ME changes knowingly or unknowingly, to WE benefit, yet always does it include the You too as before, but in a better way.

Sincerely Asking Your Source for help; You show Love within this act of trust. You show Love, when You use Love. Your Source, the Universe, by its inherent Law, faithfully responds in a way that will be noticed. But, respond it will.

Pure Love given and Love received negates the need for words, with information for the perfect solution to any situation, seeded within the interaction of Love energy.

Love sometime clarified and brought into relief, when necessary, by the Tester. If Love be taken for granted or overlooked, then possibly the Tester appears accompanied by those twin opposites of Love – fear and anger. The Tester may be viewed as the wolf that circles and scares the sheep to return to the centre of the fold again and to the Shepherd and the Source.

Romantic Love, such a beautiful reflection of the Source of Love within You and another. Glimpsed within each other, knowingly and unconsciously. How exquisite of the Source to again connect through You from someone held dear and special.

All may demonstrate faith. If You are with fear, You demonstrate faith in evil. Keep faith yet move the faith switch to Love and its one Source.

Rarely do people worry about 'We'. There is often much daily worry about 'Me'. With Love First slide to thinking 'We'.

Being of Love, increases energy. Being not of Love, decreases energy.

'Love people' - with Love, empower. 'MinusLove people' with a MinusLove condition, disempower. Love First You and so naturally you can Love All.

Materially, to have more than can be used, risks those in Your employ, those close by, are kept with less than they need. With Love First, may equilibrium be restored.

Even darkness is empowered into being by the Light and with the permission of Love. Everything is of Love and ultimately a purpose to serve Love, in Forever.

Asking

Asking of the Loving Power That Created Us and All

' Our dear Source of All in All, Life of Life, Love infinite and of Love unending; may our will be thy will, our plans be Your plans, our Love be of Your Love, May we create and decide, interact and please You, praise You and serve You with all our being in eternal gratitude and unending joy. For You have given us everything including the final freedom of free will; so free and so perfect is it, that some fully turn their backs to You while knowing You have provided everything past, present and future while loving us unconditionally, even so. We offer our free will finally, back to You with humbleness and in total gratitude throughout Forever. Forgive us, we Love You within every moment of every day of Forever Now.'

Asking : on behalf of those impaired, in pain, disconnected within and from loved ones. For those feeling no hope or future.

' With the help of Angels may they be aware of Our Creator, acknowledge their original Source and allow the Great Love beyond understanding into their core and guided to return Love direct to what they conceive The Creator to be. May they enter into dialogue Now and in their Forever. May their restoration now commence.'

Love Energy Practice

In Your stillness, sit or stand before something that is not working or being as it perhaps should. Be it a mechanism, object, body, relationship, a task to accomplish.

Empty of anger . . . forgive. No matter if it caused anguish before this moment or a threat to the future.

Now gazing, Focus Love as energy upon the object for 5 minutes as if gentle sunlight. Love from Your heart first. Calm, encompassing and continual. Attention may wander to the future or the past, or another location. Gently, return the focus of Love, back to the Here and the Now.

To increase Love energy; silently from Your heart core, invite Your own Source of Love to join with You.

After 5 minutes, send Gratitude and return to the everyday world, allowing Love energy to carry on. No need to supervise. . .

Remembering Love makes perfect, note changes now and in the days ahead.

A

Meditation

In stillness and silence be aware of just Your life breath only.

Send Love to your breath.

When ready, send Your Love to Your Source who gave You this breath.

When ready, breathe in from Your Source and breathe out Love to Your Mind and the Thoughts emanating.

When ready, breathe in and breathe out with Love imbuing the body You now reside within.

When ready, breathe in and breathe out with Love imbuing the room, building, vehicle, locality, You now reside within.

When ready, breathe in and breathe out with Love, imbuing the galaxy You now reside within.

When ready, breathe in and breathe out with Love imbuing the Universe You now reside within.

When ready, breathe in and breathe out with Love imbuing beyond the Universe into the infinite beautiful Creation of now and Forever constantly unfolding that You reside within.

When ready, breathe in and breathe out with Love to Love itself in its essence, to its Source with Gratitude, to Yourself with Gratitude and All Life with Gratitude

With Love, know that All Creation is provided to You for Love or Learning of Love. . . So that You may also . . . Love unlimited in Your Forever, Now.

Footnote

The cover photograph is of a simple wax candle with its corresponding reflection from the table surface below. Taken minutes after discussion waned regarding whether to print the received inspirations or not. The flame, a standard oval from the time of lighting, had flickered intensely, becoming far brighter. Though no apparent draught was present, this amusing new flame formed a curious short rectangle shape. It demanded a photograph. Upon enlargement, the shape and depth suggested perhaps, that of an opened book. It has never occurred since. It was taken that a sign had been duly given.

www.ingramcontent.com/pod-product-compliance
Ingram Content Group UK Ltd.
Pitfield, Milton Keynes, MK11 3LW, UK
UKHW042009190726
13854UKWH00005B/2228

9 781800 316614